Infantilisms

Infantilisms
Louis Armand

PUNCHER & WATTMANN

First published in 2024
Published by Puncher & Wattmann
PO Box 279
Waratah NSW 2298

info@puncherandwattmann.com

**NATIONAL
LIBRARY**
OF AUSTRALIA

A catalogue record for this book is available from The National Library of Australia.

ISBN   9781922571694

Cover design by Louis Armand
Printed by Lightning Source International

Acknowledgements

Thanks to David Musgrave, Ross Gillett, Pam Brown, Alex Houen, Bronwyn Lea, Toby Fitch, Pete Spence, Sarah Holland-Batt, Texas Fontanella, William Lessard, Christopher Joseph McGoff. Some of these texts have appeared, in previous incarnations, in *Meanjin, Island, Blackbox Manifold, Alienist, Cordite, Overland, Five-2-One, Entropy, Heavy Feather Review, Alien Buddha, Oz Burp, Read On, Ploise, Minarets, No Placebo, Uncolonized* (ed. Christian Patriccini), *Ashbery Mode* (ed. Michael Farrell).

Disclaimer

These poems
are entirely
works of fiction.
The language,
both literal
& figurative,
portrayed in them
is the product
of the author's
imagination.
Any resemblance
to actual language,
living or dead,
is entirely
coincidental.

Contents

*It is for childhood to preserve the social body
from contamination by the civilised classes,
by taking upon itself the performance
of all unclean & despised functions*
— *Charles Fourier*

Titanium White

winter's painted childhood was the luminous
eye wing of a trapped locust

if a moment collapses back
into its prototype

if an instant is the bow-wave
of an orphaned precession

observe this slagged rock on which
the great mandala hangs

a mind the size (93 billion lightyears)
& age (14 billion years) of the cosmos

know that we came from the sea
& are composed of water
which is dialectic

& given a blind coefficient to alter

to count at the end
as in the beginning

sacrosanct as the 4 stomachs
of apocalypse

though diminished now to pavement wraiths

choirs & bitumen sing
the perfected measure
of imperfect things

an erasure pulsing w/ capillary life

the child blinks so that
the artist
        sentimental for an ease of judgment
can make a tabula rasa of it

A Defiance of Poetry

impermanence was a beautiful thing –
the chorus of Medea
comes & goes.
fugue states in the unemployment office –
dead bones drive over the plough.

parameters & starting points:
"I" have at different times been neither
man nor woman.
(see how the wretched
of the earth ignite?)
if masked contagions
spread interference through mind-antennae.
to write is the cruellest joke.

consider the following:
it's the egg that brings closure
to life & death – quarantine
creates plague-zones, oracular signs
invisible to a sceptic eye.

nature-within-genius offers:
the oeuvre shifting from
posterity to self – hatched
in a scavenger's pit, conducively aleatory.
at this moment it assumes the pose
of an idea struggling to gasp.
("raze the idols!")

& so the day arrives before the minute-hand
strikes – hours killed slowly
expire all-at-once.
upon the primed oscilloscope

not one note too many.
& how the light
falls so slantingly on the distance that remains.

Passion Play

even the most public suffering is lived in private
joy, humiliation, which gives it the appearance
of a twelfth-century fiasco / a barricade in a
trap-street / a new decade learning to walk upright.

count to four & already victimhood becomes you
its atavistically high cheekbones / borrelitic eyes
like a hard-bitten caravanserai with the skin
of sacrificial goats / or world-beating incest

in a helix of squid-ink / bird feast primitive /
telling of empty spaces only you can see, sacred
to creatures you cannot / their universal taboo
speaks solely to a universal fact. parting the seas,

an event from an occurrence / a distinction
from senescence / a periphery from its periphery
in transient real-time, construes the baroque
anguish of second nature suicided by proficiency

or weird shrink-wrapped neurotoxins of deep-state
Godzilla revenge circuit / how forever poignant
the death of a whistleblower laid at their feet
like a rare bathmat. you were what they meant.

Metamatic

up to the critical moment
before the Fire Department w/ extinguishers & axes
a truly joyous machine
there's no denying
these are
trying times –
but tell me what good is a machine
w/ no grudge against society?

Verfremdungseffekt

(after Bohumil Hrabal)

if a man
having discovered his limits

undiscovers them
again

falling
four floors

w/ a bag of breadcrumbs
in his hand

if the pigeons
mourn over him

if the loyal dog
pisses delicately into his ear

& yawns

Conspiracy Theory
is Contemporary Genre Literature

1. the task isn't to tell the truth / but to induce
in the reader / the belief that they've discovered it

2. only the poet finds Abyssinia
inside the toe of their shoe

3. there are / worlds / where the sea / never / makes landfall

4. they dream of a sentence that can be pursued to the end w/
absolute certainty; of a word as definitive as a tombstone; of a
book after which nothing more can be said

5. silence / finally / also unheard

Logos

words can be bullets / can be homes / can be
                    spaceships / can be a triage station / a factory /
a fortress / a forest / a feast / a frailty /
                      a ferocity / a forgetting / a fin-du-monde /
that little detachable part of the body
                         wrapped up in its final breath like a gift

Humanity & the Point at Which It Disappears

in process of being refilled: the holes, painted black –
each an effulgence
    drill-bit / sump / retort
  many angles opposing
      making the first hole
    & the opposite hole
      anatomic repeat arguments –
nothing is simple here: the escape artist
on such a day
in the prehistory of an idea –
      "eyesplit of retro-
    spective luneshine…"
was life just animated photographs
    w/ button-eyes
    moth-eaten fur
      a test pilot's
      artificial leg –
  or a pea-green boat
    set upon a sea of ersatz?

too soon the negative
acceleration of mass
arrives to bring them
      back
      into its enormity

* there is a[n other] version w/ terms & conditions attached as if (~~in order to be crossed~~) some kind of unambilical line must first be drawn, then erased

20

Histories of Adversity

Be aware that the monster
may be located behind you.
Another Hamlet Machine black-&-white movie matinee
lying awake listening to the night-strangler.

A sawn-off shotgun in the woods, waves crashing
on mythomorphic rocks boiled from the sea, ill winds,
a dead seagull's eye.
                    Departure predicates necessity –
before the liberating army & boot-soles on the stairs,
drains clogged w/ scalped hair, a gramophone Chopin
plucking piano wires forever detuned no matter
how tight the years wind them.
                            All the cast-iron
laws a sung breath turns to rust upon, afraid more
of silence than of dollars (whispering the language
of the dead, while solitude exists only in *this* world).
                        But if a mountain
                        can be lured
                        to the sea,
                            why did Hannibal
                            cross the Alps
                                    one-eyed
                                    on the back of an
                                    elephant
                                            in the middle
                                            of winter?

Vague Germs of the Unknown

These relentless solitary occasions – against the wind against the wall against the sky in seas of black eyeball flotsam. All the fifth columns of all the eleventh hours. The decision as to what constitutes is difficult. Bolt-cutters, gasmask, signal flare. Does the head so easily topple off its ladder? Decrying the all-powerful words the words all-powerful: nom du père du fils & nom du mon(o)pole! Every structure has a resonant frequency at which it vibrates & blows apart. Consuming the emotional oxygens in the ovens in which they bake their seig-heiling golems. Such anomalous propositions such anonymous prostitutions. Hong Kong Beirut Santiago. Riot formations at full tilt. Brainfuse & the cultivated miracle of defunct political chatter. For sleep, continue. Each stroke's brutist cock stirring verbwise till mandalas grow out of it. Then suddenly we're touching on the poem again: psychotic ants in lockstep down the page. As the lines lengthen & the pulse quickens. The holding cell is the entire biography. Domino stack, hanging-stool. The genuine luneshine for which there's only enough evidence to convict. After a few hours the shape becomes obvious. After three days an indiscriminate loss of consciousness. There was no point resisting they said. Standard echoes slated for demolition. The Committee for Gravity Annulment in permanent session. To deplete. To gain *one more* occasion. They'd spent lifetimes refining their manifestos of radical despair under skies crossed-out: poetry was just another dispersal tactic. The whole respectable world meanwhile dreaming of god's star-shaped anus. Plastic & tinfoil. Instalment plan for lifesize replicas. Each cell was an iambic pentameter: each sonnet a cellblock. New insurrections were constantly taking shape. Anthologies of defeat charged w/ symbolic meaning. The actual possibility of the survival of the species, etcetera. They bought a ticket to China, tunnelling south. Alas, poor John, the night was unbearably long. Lining up behind the first queue that offered its services. There was no end of Literature on the subject. Case files of everything that isn't (the case). Work or nothingness, they said. Believing in order to repair, as long as the whole idea fit into an ad-break. Sleep child! The scorpions of dilemma fade into the sweatslick pillow y're forever gagging on.

Das Selbstporträt

Nor does the poem console its adversary.
The ship w/ its delicate cargo
aground on the hydrometrics of the last glacier.

In search of nothing their efforts resulted in art.
These were blueprints for ending.

Throughout the 20th century those possessing aura
took on the mantle of fabrication.

In the family-viewing section
sculptured behemoths become extinct
exactly on schedule.

The preparation of glue from bones for example
transponders radars conical middens of fissile junk.

These erotic petrifications
make a wandering unrest of the watcher's
pinhole eyes.

Or a shipwreck on the moon
serves as a protagonist in the absence of any other.

Its relics cleansed of the odour of veneration,
the question about the basis of writing
now begins to find its answer.

Artist's Head Imprisoned in Plexiglass

It's the future	In the future
& you're already dead – an itinerant	already dead, you're an itinerant
anachronism	anachronism
inside a vacuum tube,	in a vacuum tube
inside the shape of facts-as-given.	no-one will ever switch on.
When's an idea not its own medium?	Construed fact-wise,
Certain there're /only/	these aren't the only
questionable things –	questionable /things/ – the presence
though less puzzled by them	of the camera, for example,
than they are by you.	nautilus to its own inhabiting image.
The cameras are turned to ensure	Harmless as it seems,
a reluctance more picturesque.	history still revolts you.
On the third day,	Like a dog-hair coat,
the news you'd forgotten, returned –	like a contracted zero-hour.
gripped by fear	This is a calculated
of the crucial	emotional response –
/missed moment/ –	a /change in emphasis/.
like the cryogenic avatar	But salvaged from reflections in an
who embarrasses us in dreams.	/empty/ screen,
What dark /art/ possessed it?	who will fathom it?

Beckmannesque

Purple falls unripe from haunches
blacked against a redoubt.
A sea without chairs,
magic diagrams
counterclockwise.
Each additional stroke, gouging new injuries
from old injuries,
              foretells the
        distressed eye
                  of the netted
                    fish.

Life on Mars

poetry isn't of its time: tele-
scoped into the evoked
space – a planet whose drift,
fitted w/ a contrary
screen / as from afar
the ancient volcanoes –
rivers within rivers /
granted, being human
had its advantages:
blameworthiness, for example.
y'd wish their god
existed just to see
the looks on their faces –
but from the moment they
stepped out of the
module / nothing
was ever going to be the same
again

Last Words

To expect the worst doesn't make you prepared –
whipping the sea so as not to make a fool of it.
Fatalism came easier to people used to standing naked in line.
Only foreigners write poetry.
Daily reports arrive of bacteria billions of years old –
reminding of that moment in *Slaughterhouse Five* (the movie)
when Prague, pretending to be Dresden,
turns into a pile of rubble & the SS men
in dubious black put a bullet in the good guy.
A flowering error like excrement or fidelity.
We force puzzles from the preceding echo –
mining the untapped potential of lunar real-estate &
prestidigitated other worlds.
Once upon a time, a felled tree carried the giant stones, the ships,
paved a continent – they accomplished all this
w/ neither axle nor wheel.
Complacency is still warmer back where you can see it.
Wide of the mark, the fatuous understatement
still intercepted their escape plan.
The last word wasn't better than the rest, it just had circumstance
on its side.

Redheads

Freiheit ist immer die Freiheit
des Andersdenkenden
　　　　— Rosa Luxemburg

It's always the student
who kills the teacher.
Or vice versa.

Believing in undiscovered
fossil remains
in a canal on Mars.

You light a match,
a "safety match,"
but the fire doesn't know that.

What lunacy has occurred
in the world
while you slept?

The mind's mazurka
& the mazurka
of the turning spheres.

Chances were
the alternatives got there
before you did.

Letter on Alienism
(to Jésus-Bernstein Pataquouèrique)

The sacrificial lamb. The death of personal myths.
All endings are portentously written –
plunging back to an alien, inanimate youth,
of dancing men in Archimedes' bathroom?
No proof was ever needed – the world
there long before you doubted it.
In truth you concern yrself most
w/ the spirit of demoralization,
but god isn't the one asking the questions.
The silvery moon's absurd in the sea
w/out the red-handed hygienic animal to seize it.
Four billion lightyears away in the infinite
wherewithal, an odalisque's mouth makes an expressive study
of a living or dying attitude –
unable to justify committing words-to-page?
One iota's owed so much for so little.
Many other unsolved mysteries in the solar system:
the "wider life-spectrum" as reported on TV news.
Did continuity offer a solution?
Like playthings-of-memory to the sleep-disturbed,
I & my autism crave witness
only of that which craves not us,
building a fallout shelter against dark-matter relativity –
a bitten tongue or a terrain of impaired vision –
& not the offended angels who exist
by antiphrasis. The way Christ is always shown
w/ a head like a solemn oyster.
He balances neurons on a pin. We've all seen his
contemplated toe through nod-off eyes
that don't know where the next fix is coming from,
only that it must.

Sonnet for Bill Berkson (R.I.P.)

Sunday morning 7th Avenue a woman & dog
polychromed in recycled Duane Reade –
coffee makes anti-heroic counterstances
$8.50-per-hour hinting at but not showing.
Steam rises on the intersection, the definitions
they taught at school to act out in slow
orderly motion: getting to the opposite
streetside cld be a life's labour. Rubber soles
collecting rain – a teeth-brushing Picasso fixated
by the mirror's inefficiencies – chalklines on pavement
beckoning like a lost half. Dreamed
of obsolescence but not the epilogue:
brownstones w/ yellow blinds, a barber's pole,
a hydrant – the subway grinning while it weeps.

Sonnet for Hugh Clarence Ultan

Who if they cannot love the police could answer
the stairs' hegemonic laughter?
Though I, being the dour childeater of yr dreams,
shall sanction all –
protean as a many-layered bride,
allegorical as spaceflight or the eye
of a self-fellating snake.
The timbre, for example, of nightwhile urinations.

Often for reasons unknown a storm abruptly vanishes,
becomes meteorology. Thinning sea-hair & renal
calculus. The dead forms are carving America
into our spines, but who will mime
the chorus of its & their declining
power? Yrs was to be an unruleable country.

Sonnet for Iris Clert

This is a sonnet if you say it isn't.
This is a sonnet if you say it isn't.
This is a sonnet if you say it isn't.
This is a sonnet if you say it isn't.

This is a sonnet if you say it isn't.
This is a sonnet if you say it isn't.
This is a sonnet if you say it isn't.
This is a sonnet if you say it isn't.

This is a sonnet if you say it isn't.
This is a sonnet if you say it isn't.
This is a sonnet if you say it isn't.
This is a sonnet if you say it isn't.

This is a sonnet if you say it isn't.
This is a sonnet if you say it isn't.

(Non)Fiction Sonnet

a poem is (not) an
object it can (not) be bombed
nullified anatomized
reformed bought
sold faked
forgotten buried

in a mouth in a museum vault
in a hole on a desert island
in the small print in a subcortex
in a book no-one can read
in an intestinal tract
in a beam of laserlight

directed at a point arbitrarily remote
on the other side of the cosmos

Transit Duty
(i.m. Michel Butor)

It's not what's past that casts its light, sordid, on our final hours. A
colossus straining w/ arms out horizontally night & day in
laws up to its groin. Crash-landing an autonomous god in
stop-motion was an unknown philosophy. Wind-worn our
ill will's hilarity scornfully grins – hurrah! for today's riot
of humiliations, thanks is paid. At first guilty, but who'd
insist? Ballooning to unconscious fog, clouds, icy rain,
inhuman combats. Flat on our backs, on our stomachs,
happily in spring mud crawling – woman & man, yard
upon suppurating yard, instant upon staccato instant. Vast
migrations of guppy, frog, lizard, dog, kangaroo, gorilla,
all or anything forcing fast aboard, always in co-conspiring
mirrors. And what did *you* do? Night slips a hand into its bag
of tricks. Cicadas sing, summoning abysms too far to cross.
Our commandant anxiously awaits a last signal – to stand
fast, to fall back – now or midnight or untold tomorrows.
But all is cold as radio static, no word mars its uniformity.
Only, far off, solid ground rising in furious candour.

Ulysses at Quarter-to-Eight
(i.m. Harry Mathews)

These things were clues, unfolded from a shrunken head,
    the stentorian cell beneath the slide, dissuaded
    trilobites under the procrustean bed.
All through the night he held on by his eyelids.
Tomorrow isn't for song, they said, though not out-of-
    character w/ their enigmatic standards.
Pattern was everything.
The coiled walls of illuminated insurrection.
Some avidities burn in the wrong transistor, causing fallout
    to false accords.
The earnest anarchist primes his bomb, though for you the
    unanswerable, the many shrug, it's not the first time
    they've been peddled a scheme.
A Swedish ingénue sniffing glue in Portobello suede.
Tropical pressure in the Alfred North Whitehead.
How much to be desired was the unbuttoned accordion,
    the cold side of pork roulade, the jellied seaweed
    purveying undomiciled bliss?
The sky was a flyspecked jigsaw puzzle.
As long as the dissolved soap refused to harden, they knew.

The Dream of the Fisherman's Wife
in the Mind of the Fisherman

Time & tide lock the doors, launch the ships.
Under the sea their fallout shelter –
                always voices whispering:
"no man ever born," they said.

The monster chained to his leg – its lunate eye,
slipping through nets, skirting the precipices.

A fine settling of mist –
                to this purpose & no other;
the promised eugenic & no other.

The days, he came to believe, weren't long enough.
Dark energy accelerating the universe,
building the crisis roster.

Deutschland in Autumn,
the old Confucian proverb:
                tous les chevaux du roi
in a ditch
at the bottom of the sea –
& nothing to drink.

Another night hauling in the lines. There are oceans
full of keyholes, primordial mirrors.

Roy Orbison is crying & the people also are
crying in Ho Chi Minh City.

                Listen!
                Venezuela is talking in its sleep.

Well every American president
deserves to go hungry at least.

Orizaba (Hart Crane)

A few moments before.
Noon, after
removing his coat –
      the burnt pages
& buried passages
were stopgaps.
              From walking up & down
      making
      counter-
          points to
              derricked sky.
To drown must be horrible.
Bolted to the river, fractioned, un-
immaculate:
      the death
      to be free
          of death.
        Or not
            free, but
                disobliged.

The Sun is in the Bowl

Even w/ good intentions
the world grows older
as it grows further away.
A rubber shower-mat
they build meanings on
at the same time as it
slips & you dance.
Not hearing what it couldn't
see. Not seeing.
I've kept what secrets I can.
The politics of photographs
promises not to, if you
don't. Repairing the scenery
when nothing was broken.
The preceding moment
was the picture of happiness.
Were you ever as violent
as you remember being?
The day the war began
& the child, lost
between goal posts,
after the penalty was kicked.
Stretched beyond the
blurred edges, a hundred
years float by into the
dead-ball zone.

Eye is Non-Refundable Index of Mind Condition

And if the idiot persists in the ideogram,
               as the cuckoo persists
               in the factory clock?
She sides w/ the enemy, always, yr
               sentimental schaden Freude.
Shouting over rooftops
               they discovered too late
               the source of its curious technique.
Or it promises nothing but a secret occasion
               to remain.
Consider the ways
               a plastic reproduction seascape
               is left behind.
An excessive vagueness of sky,
               wave-lines,
               or a scorched bird
               marking ten-minutes-to-ten.
Remember everything: the organ-donored
               paralysis, even
               their bones swallow the light.
Beauty grows from reality into life
               in the duress of it.

The Night Train's Vagrancy

Now winter's curtain is parted,
the eye smarts
in its precipitous weather

& all the pale sinking
Virgins of Guadalupe
are like fingers rehearsing an étude.

To be shown the generosity
shown to others
isn't the lot of the pamphleteer

who hurries to amend
the nursery tale
from which the unhappy children

fail to emerge.
For months the bars had been
on the wrong side

of the windows,
though from his locked room
he can see things

most people can't.
It was discovered
the future is moving

faster towards us
than we are towards it.
Thinking to cut it off at the pass,

the cavalry major
rode into the scenery
while the besieged music

burnt its last offerings
& calmly sipped Kool-Aid
in the jungle heat.

St Paul Shipwrecked with a Burning Snake

The heat breaks everything down.
      Slumped into a corner
a dog rains on yr hat
stirring the air noncommittally.
      What else does a man w/ a
beam in his eye have to say,
but don't surrender till you see
the colour of their money?
      The sea runs out shallow for miles
like a lizard ogling a fly
forever out of reach, or a fly quizzing
a shape in the shadow of a rock,
which in the legend had already become it.

The Regress of Myth

To challenge art in its patrimonial dimension,
a city walked off & abandoned itself.

No-one speaks of revolution around here.

Skydiving into the Rio de la Plata,
red-winged urn / one-eyed / tongue
nailed to forehead. Intention is an ice-pick
rising to its antipolitical task –
symmetry eats its bleeding heart.

In the omniscient courtyard the Artist labours
over his sentimental allegorical breakfast.

Broken yolks are as a child to sullen
policemen – their yellow, raining
alienisms upon the workday menagerie,
exhorts the wallpaper to ever greater effort.

The Murder of Rosa Luxemburg

To this add the perils of revisionism
whose illustrated children's stories
were really about murdering Jews –
          like Kafka's 3 sisters
          & Freud's 5 sisters
          whose brilliance & disaster
          led not to insurrection.

Far off in the eventful world
the old engine sat on the turntable
waiting to be sent back down the line –
          chugging along the coast
          stopping at all the villages
                    before it comes
                    to port.

Tom Raworth's Blues

Does the poem bypass the Organization of Meaning? Swiftly,
in the second line, comes "introspection" – which is the idea
of an entered mind, apparently. An inner-ear speleologist.
At a cursory glance it resembles Henry James' rug
thrown over a garble of mis-penned verbiage. Then
there's the sinister windmill burning outside the window.
Quixotes in toy fire trucks weeeeeeeeeeeeeeeeeeeeee!
Primitive as these literal pleasures are they're no mind-readers.
Hiding the not-yet-perished cell-motes in a jar, in a drawer,
on the remote off-chance. Not all keep their ugly lexicons stashed.
In the meantime one travelled – a summary of forceful
quizzical luddites, senescent out of boredom. Money-curse
not diversified refusal. A difficult adagio. Bert Brecht also died
decrying the Organization Man's flagrantly hacked sub-ego.
It keeps things afloat that don't exist. Or they do
but underwhelm initially like the opposite of hypochondria.
Consolation was missionary grift.

The Unity of Means

Where're we when we're here? By now so many shouts
in the street & still no god.
Yes we've objected. No
we haven't burnt their cities down.
A mirror was once an ape's philosophic toy,
eine kleine Nachtmusik. The antic sun
falls out windows, it's freezing.
        Not by choice of circumstance are they dead.
Instructed to correct in the repeat sequence, the twittering
machines were painted photographs
of an "evolutionary event."
        There're things we don't have names for,
        either.
           All night
           the empty lift
           traversed
           the height
           of the glass
           tower:
                a flickering
                signal pattern
                      in a
                      broken
                      TV.

Statements of Purpose

what form will the final witness take?
if a tree falls in the absence of a forest.
here always a god is dying,
a piece of congealed myth disturbed
by the swirling dust of a stochastic neural analogue.

backed into a corner
the voluptuously coiling octopus vents its ink.
they built walls to keep people in.
the torpor against struggle,
the cancer of opposites.

at their photovoltaic rostrums,
murmuring priests conduct the microspheric symphony
bursting in the lung. c'est fini, l'art!
storm, whirlwind, earthquake.

in the end all they wanted was to abolish time:
the *crime passionnel* of the discarded element.
one by one its extraneous plots
"like" phosphorescent nightbirds.

if by seeing, confusion is heightened:
tongue-torn charting the stars
in the attic, the great rivers of the sub-basements.
no creation w/out first a victim.

& set out upon a raft across the onyx-veined blemish
of a convalescent's eye:
motion, silence, at the confluence
of centrifugal life.
there are no inexplicable frequencies.

La Vie Sentimentale

love referred us to commodities, my last
memory of a butter saw – so young so beautiful,
continence makes us houseproud.
at 8 o'clock it was the geneticists' turn
scattering grey sunflower seeds – still
no sign of the sun – to widen the contingencies,
the lighthouse beach, the high altar,
life w/out knowing. we lived a film made for TV –
smoke wld rise & wreathe the penises
& roads fretted w/ mimosa. open all the windows!
hot wind swaying the flywire, a taxi at the door
frantic to see other pictures. nudity, boredom
is a failed state on the road to autocracy –
another wave of etceteras to replace the loyal
interpreter w/ a talent for grift. everyone
gets bitten at least once, their departing voices said.

Home Movie

A shop window a piece of cheese labelled CHEESE
some dying cypress trees – the obvious conclusion
is a scenery of deliberate malaise in which
the sun hangs like a grey lightbulb. As once
primitives brought forth tungsten from their caves.
Thrust anxiously forward the camera is a body
blinking back at itself in time-delay a landscape
w/ hearing aid on a spectrum of nondescript.
Swimming parties beneath a bridge. Cropped heads
oblique. All this told by an upsidedown clock
in a room the shape of smeared mascara –
hours nakedly in disarray. A square of light opens
a door. Cld this be the entrance y've been waiting for?
Time may tell when only these 4 walls can listen.

That Perilous Night

into the human situation / a wheeled arena
      meaningless in themselves
      instantly fascinated skyscrapers leap
black arrows & hands
mysteriously from darkness
whose energy
painted over w/ great heat
continues to exert
      I reached the conclusion that
      several winters'
      contemplation boxes
            knotholes
            of infectious inactivity
            plotting revenge
      but if you don't change yr mind
      about past art
      as an advertisement of all that's sick
like stopmotion war footage
or America
or unbreathable 4-colour separation process
      any sort of transparency
      watered from above
      before it reaches 33 seconds w/out
      striking a note or
      penetrating the world
            because finally in plain view
            is already something done
            no longer something doing

How to Build a House

Plunging monuments to Usherise: basefall, subproletarian –
an abscessed plastic accoutrement of the respiratory tract.
If by describing.
                     Artisanal, being veins of glass
                     headlong into senseless metaphor –
another electron run to ground: "effects have no surfaces" (Dürr).
Playing one gridlock against another –
bloodshot Oedipus-obsessives
gaming Iron Dome negative dialectic.
                                   The opposite is also true.
Their latest pilot-plan's component hypothesis,
incendiary balloons & self-hate –
                    even a child knows
                            where the catastrophic pieces lie.

Landscape with Figures
Mostly Living or Recently Deceased

the mysteries of oxygen
make ruthless advance
upon the scenery

more sombre variations
on the theme of birds
an emotional commonplace

of the agitated observer;
of the immovable father

even the monumental fermions
petrified, residual;
diurnal, ambivalent

having witnessed
all there was to see
it was time for the spectacle
to move on

Apophenia

the ten
      dency
           of un
                related
                    things
to per
      ceive
           connect
                ions &
                    meaning
i love
you
they say

Iliad

overcast & then went down to the storied embankment
call-numbered dog-eared –

turn the page: how blank
the façades. born of no ironic effect
in catalogued mute dismantling
what's written – the 7
forms of hubris 3 ages
of anxiety metaphor's orphanage.

mouths yawn impatient
for their turn. will it rain? (will it ever rain again?)

                    having set out to conquer
                    they observed the river's
                    somnolent effect.

            each leaf
      as it settles
                    a humid sigh

Achille Lougé (Cailhau)

Le point la ligne la lumière
the purple sky the blue Pyrénées –
dans une village de la Malepère
the domineering mother rations the soup
an orange slice soaked in tea.
There are seagulls in search of a sea
as if a hundred years had passed
& only a white expanse to show for it.
Is this what art is? Une maison
des perruches? Un garde-fou?
Sonnettes de nuit ou l'objet amoureux
d'une flèche du Parthe? Déjà vu?
Poison swims through the eye to create
a point-of-view hidden in plain sight.
Another garden of unearthly delights
& ravished turpentines to judge
from appearances. *Oedipus at Colonus*
the apocryphal last scene: interior night.

Dictation Lessons

Days vanish. The cat-eye in the corner
sneaking after you. And on & on.
You spend money to feel less lonely.
Diet pills & morning passes so smoothly!
But can anything be summed up
that isn't dead? A ship in dry-dock,
a house on blocks, the industriousness
of a city full of cartoon clocks?
Any child cld've written this.
Subworld locutions pretending to be echoes
(so that only you understand them).
Desire, necessity, all the dilemmas on which
others took a stand, or failed to.
You think of them sometimes,
too busy expostulating to ever hear
what's left unsaid. Silence is golden.

Éloge de l'amour

there are things an artist shouldn't know –
worlds fall apart each instant

> in a sliding
> equilibrium

ch.1: in which history gives acct of itself –
woman & man

> in a foreign city:

untenable constructions
during the course of night –
examples include (lest forgotten):
law & thus death
poetries

> of industrial
> azur –

writing must place unreasonable demands

in fear – words the least foreground –
prosceniumed battalions winter their soprano
les méconismes
de la vie mentale:

the hidden spectacle
of wave-function collapse, or

an erotics of vanishing
in short, art could almost not exist:

> abandon all
> positions, it says,
> the plumed serpent
> sheds its scales –

are these the dawning etceteras?
fewer & lesser
fever & what follows

barricaded – as in the larynx – a door unhinged
how it does / decides what it does:
                              still something
                    will resist

30 January

One's born every minute.
A smudged hole to peer out because sleepless.
Snow on the river
around the hulls & pitches.

In some parallel maybe dimension
the railbridge shouts
                    Bon anniversaire!
And you're skating over nostalgia's thin ice
w/ all the aplomb
of a ten-storey ballerina.

Dragooned ducks ogle from the wings.
It's the Radetzky March,
                    three anapests & one iamb
            clapping & stomping.

Oh how the green slender hands
play the tram wires.
Chagall horses leap in a sky where
everything's not owned,
not named.
"Hello," they say, "are you coming too?"

Myth of the Aviator

warps & wasps of the turtle pond:
                conurbations reflect concentrically
        carp gulping the horizon's march

or the calculated end of an illness
                running its course
        backwards into the bamboo thicket

& a sky blank as August that
                resembles more than anything else
        an antique photograph of itself

X is Proof of Life's Perseverance

Evolution went off with aplomb / hand's end in compound eye
a thin cosmic rain frayed binocular / face-overs in a 3-dimensional.
These are the reality labs, turnpikes / of videotape war-game
stanzaic micropore, power-tooled / on fixed-odds white suburbanism.
Afloat inside its opaque substance / reblend sales pitch to brainstem
adrenal flux upping the ante / dreams of x-rayed South Pacific.
This ersatz death by viral delivery plan / such hypergothic suns
make anguish their daily meat / in skies adrift on black pollen:
their *petites fleurs du mal* disport timelapse / naked or frozen
in scrupulous attitudes of respect / for the cosmic masterplan.
But we must breathe more than ontic metadata / the situation
"couldn't last" / the times were "unbearable." Oh how even a bouquet
of misery gives tarnish a new face / & god something to live for.

Methamphetamine Landscapes

night falls on hydrostatic moons,
a symphony of lithiums

display cabinets w/ preserved specimens:
& made a sail of their skin, bone mast, hull

the litmus of end times.
Here gravity concedes!

w/ the tenacity of a sea urchin,
the trigonometric spirit moved upon the waters

the world on its head
translated about an axis

so too the shadows dance in silent mandalas
their joie de mourir

Closing Time at "Alcatraz" (St Mark's Place, 1995)

Mugshot artist down to her last trick – Identikit Man –
the Tightrope Kid – grown tired of régimes searching
her vagina for their alter-egos. A window onto the soul
isn't the poetic sublime you commit crimes for, she said.

Playing a Tuli Kupferberg air-guitar in protest
at the solemnity of art's demise.
The closest point to chaos is still further than you can see,
in Kropotkinite gloom gaslit for the occasion.

Does the cost of remembering better times
make them more valuable?
Or just shorter in supply?

Nations, like infants, are constantly groping
for a language they can suck dry w/ impunity.
Even the least paid demand cries out to be fought.

40,000 Years of Modern Art

...the same tendencies in Enlightenment philosophy:
the mathematical model of human understanding,
the absolute opposition of subject & object,
& the conception of truth as unchanging...
— Pericles Lewis

Aggregated into time, the traps learnt to scent you before they're set. A room inside an echo, a rude observation post hand-worked like an original UFO. Progress, its very blankness implies it. There was to be no more depiction – people had died for less. Lying there w/ the vapid eroticism of a détourned prodigal, telling you there is no war. Strange fruit hangs from an insubstantial threat, resolutely *tabula rasa*. Just as Damascus is far from where *it* seems – even the walls of its irreducible reality are TV static. How late still to be counted as having arrived – & now the silos, too, gaping omnivorous & starved at the sky like a lost golden age. There's always more pathos in denial – Europe after rain, the first conquistador, Carthage before the fall. Instructed to "give in," things wouldn't be different w/ a shared point of view – the children you've been spying on all winter, taking their game behind doors to inner soviets of the mind's eye. Deliberately the finger hesitates over the switch, awaiting the signal for the ominous coincidence to occur.

Politique Cubiste

attempts

      to stage

           a con

sensus

      re pre   sent ing

      a   s
      l   i
      l   d
                e
                s

Quixote

this / tilted / world / is / no / windmill

A Valentine

in two days two chickens laid two eggs,
forty Flying Fortresses
seventy miles from Dresden,
as upon one foggy winter's night
in 1972
a stewardess from 30,000 ft
over a pine forest in Bohemia:
this was later revealed to her in a dream

From Quarantine

Europe after the rain –
a package of gunpowder tea,
postcards from Bergamo,
carnivale masks
on dead trees.
              They're postponing everything, only
solitude went to the head of the queue.
              A self-portrait wld be
the last thing you wrote:
                              Dear, when you stood
breathless atop the stairs but failed to fall?
"Our world" never was, it will not pain it
to burn. See
              how they have finally
                              favoured the weak?

Everything Outside the Poem
is Part of Its Meaning
(i.m. Stephen Rodefer)

At the same time you breathe out as in. These stops, valves,
personal mountains of collective molehills. He came
to prefer his incompletions, saying a forward posture isn't
the prerequisite of thought. Reaching for the last length
out-gasped, a listener among the nucleotides.
Lost in the afterglow of melted xmas trees, it was a moot
consideration of maps, it was Anthony Braxton *For Alto*,
it was bleeding fish in a solution of analgesic.
Just how bright do the headlights get? Prague in spring,
an upstairs room w/ dirty underwear hung on a line.
A sentence, a semblance, a sentience. It happened so quickly:
You're fake, he said, I don't believe y're you, pulling coloured
handkerchiefs from breast pocket 6 yards long.
He do the Wilhelm Meister in many wrong steps:
I've survived therefore I am! But whether or not
the world receives these mind transmissions, what it sees
belongs to the fine print of necessity. Evil, for example.
(It was a point in history when they neglected to lock their
presidents up at night.) Which goes some way towards,
but only partially. Displaying a sound theoretical mind,
he knew how to drink. *Pour en finir avec le jugement de Paris.*
There's more to it than just winding a mechanism, they said,
but would he? Love came & went, there were arrangements,
debts, gainsayings: a ship at port, an astronaut's umbilicus,
the mythical airlock. Always one more than you expect.
In protest the dead poet softshoes it to the bank.
As an ingrown sanctity it left a certain amount to be desired:
they'd either pin a medal on him or call it art.
Even the weather that time of year was conspiratorial.

It's Only Terminal if You Can't Sleep It Off

Old woman in black who held yr arm
crossing 14th St & all the diners that shut down talking about
Ravel or lotus blooms or the redhead
in Washington Sq with green parrot tattoo on shoulder
listening to the jazz. Dogs but no children – a failed
grace in all domesticated things. Giant
with saxophone coughs unassuming, midget chessmen
taking not one step in any direction
without preamble. The crowd making diligent
non-conformist sidesteps – fuck the distinction of
getting there, you only teach by example.
Unscrambling the Minute-Man babble, over there
a blue TV head laughing mute – reformed pin-eyed junkies –
the bored Quixotes of Bleecker St.
Possibility doesn't suicide itself for what's best.
Finding yr next idea in a 99¢ store,
first drawing lines on paper with pencil & ruler or sometimes
not ruler & without pencil. It comes down
to the thread of something, believing all these years
you turn clockwise to open, now the exceptions
come in volumes eight inches thick.
Giant washing-machines stacked against the sky, immense
people smelling of tongue liquid. They build
statues out of principles you can wander round inside
for dollars at a time. Geography may always be willing
but real estate knows where to draw the line.
Used to be progress was taking a wrong turn
& winding up in a desperate neighbourhood, but now they've
got people trained for that.
Why come so far when there's no going back?

The Road Out

1. Imperial Hotel, Coonabarabran (August, 2015)

Smoke clears to anaesthesia – invisible particles
grafted, biopsied into mosaic. The observatory's
charred perimeter turning a frozen crow-eye
at nebulous space. You made a decision
       to start out but never arrive – becoming
the last Mogul Emperor, the first proto-Elamite.
Childhood is the old carpet you wrap a god's corpse in.
       You've since learnt that periscope trick,
seeing into far corners, dark stars, the tinted cosmic lens.
Spectrographs of a currawong's satiric lament.
       In this last sleeping place, it says,
all the mattresses have come unsprung.
But that a pyre burn & be not consumed,
was construed miraculous.

2. *Red Landscape* (Fred Williams, 1981)

The eyes' traction veers off, red on red –
turn the page, a promontory cuts the horizon,
       fence lines, a distributive graph. But the road
takes you only so far – subliminal to the
gibber plain, the inland sea.
       Many means of escape have been proposed,
exhibited in museums. The vertical monotony
of progress: relay stations into the next mapless beyond –
       some distantly observed earthrise, heading west
through Martian outcountry. Barium heat &
fishbowl life-support system. The percussion section
       throttles down to a sustained chord, a stilled
furore of occasion – ticking off the intervals in seachange
doppler effect – the conductor asleep in the passenger seat.

3. *View of the Western World* (John Olsen, 1956)

The constructed travesty of a landscape
flows out to embrace you. Stark,
obdurate. A broken fence
recounts the arrival in boats.
      We are, to them, a succession of winters.
Antique firewood from subtle boxes.
The mind in repose
shakes its chains –
its language translates nothing.
      It is neither the death of sleep
nor the wild altitudes
of a misplaced shoreline.
      Salted & stored in the lightless cave,
a desert is a returning sea that never does.

4. Clifton Pugh, *Mural* (Tibooburra, 1976)

Driving at the moon, you are the wheeled
fulcrum on which this red earth turns.
      Mineral eye, shingle-tongue,
kilned in the dissolving saltpan,
in the lithopone sky.
      First light of the ancient space mariners.
A boy on a roadside, divining-rod in hand,
absorbed in the full knowledge –
alien as fossil footprints on the moon,
as Kandinsky.
      The granites make black holes in the wide
scrubbed brushstroke – a mask with eyes.
      To bury the namesakes,
to invite the question without asking it.

5. The Dark Cut (Cameron Corner, SA, NSW, QLD)

Its blood eye watches even around corners
where there're none. The flat of two vast
intersecting planes, red & black,
a gibbous lunatic twin ogling back.
       The dog fence whittles the wind for miles.
A surveyor's totempole declares invisible
boundary lines, dust dances its funereal rites.
       You paint a tin shack with bowsers into the picture
as proof of something –
like the gate you pass through,
like the dog with the stone in its mouth & red neckerchief.
       But the road out was always a gauntlet
between the eyes' onrush & unyielding.
Them & us. One after another.

Plato in the Antipodes

it began by all accounts w/ a cave.
the cruel beauty of the enemy
arrives as if by accident.
though they are dilettantes in irony.
fixed in a glassy stare the heliometric
property rite the mineral precision
dissolving in lakes of avidity.
& yet – & *yet* – WHAT IS POETRY?
the gaslight at the end of the tunnel
the algorithmic motherload.
w/ god on their side they came
to exterminate night:

>   blue glittering in domed sky
>   the lead-footed fatalisms tread

Saramago

A children's story must be simple
        & contain a moral even
        the edifiable can extract,
        like the mineral wealth
        of an unknown island.
Yet those who cry paradox
        desire only on occasion
        to be taken literally.
Just as a story with two halves
        is a manifold in another
        dimension. Walking without a map
        through the museum of barred exits.
Chastised at birth, their politics
        were simple: to be loved
        by the phraseology of command.
Behind every god is a mother
        patiently repairing the damage.
Innocence, too, knows
        the pleasures of signification,
        the melancholy of the child
        taught to unread everything.
A truth must be as simple
        as the apocryphal masses
        who only dream in advertising copy.
Because it is sinful to take
        comfort from untaxable labour,
        a children's story must be
        a crime joyfully committed,
        indebted to no moral.

Riot at the Hydromajestic

The calm uninquisitive barman handtowel-over-shoulder
framed reproduction of *The Fighting Temeraire*
dim, halfreflected, polished tile & bottleglass:
three versions of the protagonist in a lifeboat
staggering towards Salamis / refuge island / duplicating machine
head-to-foot swathed in hairofthedog.
Once more the spurious air of impartiality –
feigning reprieve from the worst-to-come.
Imaginary friends find comfort among children & the insane.
The barman's backwards grin, the irrefutable radio static –
soon entire edifices come crashing down.
Thus is desolation as inseparable from life
as a fugitive from the exultation of preparedness –
ready to leap from the poem's last line & abandon everything.

Truck & Trailer Approaching a City
(Jeffrey Smart, 1973)

Europe in a thousand container terminals –
the sat-nav recalibrates, the one language:
tollgate, tunnel, interchange. Who knows
which roads get switched in the confusion?
This welfare city or that doppelgänger
on the other side – this night or some other night.
Mindless in roadhouse parking lot,
hypno radio-voices spiral out of headlights
hard as methedrine. The closely-observed
& freely aleatory coffee grounds you devise
into apocalypse-edge visions. Patsy Cline
& border guards & fake inventory. A hundred
more miles of the hungry tank before neon
& 4:00 a.m. imitation snakeskin walls,
KY & stale aerosol. An hour's sleep beside an
identikit deadeyed blonde till the clock
switches back again to the angry white line,
& you roll to play, & the blacktop bleeds you dry.

The Silence of Martin Heidegger
(after Jorge Semprun)

how a body grows vague –
forest w/out birds
schön war die Zeit –
entering the territory
of ancient death (the executioner's
mouth cratered black)
ah! the Schadenfreude
of a mother's tongue
in lurid emotion
at the prodigal's return

there are consequences
they've paid no heed to –
voices surge across the sky
(a wide halfmoon on a dull
sheet of ground glass)
back & forth
as in Aeschylus –
the weeping masks of a mis-
begotten joke
          told once too often

Arts of Resurrection

to live means to be sick a long time — Plato, *Phaedo*

1. & then something happened. the stream wending
beneath the road, a collapsed railbridge, rats
spectating from diluvian rubble. today of all days.
was "impossible" imagining cinema without guns?
war without cameras? every god's an anachronism.
the sound of the cataract inside the ear,
of violence committed by an empty stomach.
there are dangers inherent in all coalitions.
uncurbed the lifeblood flows direct from its source
while tears hasten to perform their sorry deed.
not taxes nor revolutions belong to paupers.
now they're burning the holy relics just to stay warm:
buried alive y'd at least stand a chance.
poetry wld be more humane, but is already dead.

2. something crawling on the bed cut from
their agenda. mission control in meltdown.
that naked twisted thing, made example
by resembling (a) proof, (b) psychology.
island peering closer a living monument,
overzealous, perhaps words not finished after all.
a shell that contains a spirit on a wheel.
or nothing to fear nothing to come, weighs long after:
there were listening devices disguised as literary devices.
the symbiosis of past & future walks through walls
like a Colombian hit-squad purchased duty-free.
let us sing the triumph of the market economy!
at first they spent much time agreeing on a story,
then decided just to invent it as they went along.

Impressionism

When prison poets grow old
wanting respectability & morning opens out
west through Streeton country
to abandoned mock-heroic gold towns
& funfair Jerilderies,
the yellow-spreading patchwork
of decades-old airfreshener,
& rail-lines & swamps – turning state's witness
against all the retaliatory landscapes
hung from high horizon-lines
like meatworks carcasses –
perched stool-pigeonesque
among the anonymous eaters
of fish-&-chips, steak sandwiches & souvlakis –
shoulder to shoulder
muttering of the bad times,
obdurate as a muddied green-brown sky
of invaded peripheries:
ideally there would've been
no witnesses to metaphor's death,
but these aren't ideal times.
Intended otherwise,
the poem becomes a coded sum
of unaccountable things,
confessing w/ artless force
to lifelong inadequacies –
nor is the sunset it fails to describe
the candid or faithless picture you'd expect,
but spills out across the flat
the way words do
after a sentence in solitary confinement,
as if to take in everything.

Nelson Algren's Lament

December in Chicago, drinking the black surf under the pier –
the sky's a rotten liver, it's cocktail hour, there's a
rusted palm tree on the beach & y're hanging in it.

It's the old women on the stairs again talking in yr sleep,
like ocean sounds & highways, & it's cold being rained on
by every dog on the street, but to open yr eyes
first y've got to widen the polarities.

Well anyone can be existential w/ the lights out, he said,
but the telephone was just a jilted lover on the make
& he'd run out of change. He was a pork-pie-&-vest guy,
arms jacked back like Joe Cocker at the bar making
stutter-step holding patterns while the "Coloured Grrlz" sang
Everyone's a winner, baby, everyone's a Winnebago…

It was Jim Crow on the South Side playing lynchmob saxophone,
& Frankie Machine & the cigarette girl, & Betty Lou at the
8th street No-Tell. Y'd've written it all down but yr arm
was full of lead – what comes of being subproletarian in bed.

Because it's midnight on the TV & word had got around
about December in Chicago & the body on the pier – & there's
questions to be answered but no-one left to hear,
they've all gone south to Mexico in aviators & moustaches,
& the bozos on Memorial Day quote O'Henry to the masses.

Because it's midnight on the TV, yes the reruns were atrocious,
& the sentimental migraine pours its story down yr throat,
& the pool balls all resent you, & the barstools sit & gloat.

Gulag Blues

Well I woke up this morning in a stranger's gulag clothes,
I've got gulag in my underwear & gulag up my nose,
I've got gulag halitosis & a gulag in my brain,
this gulag hypothalamus is driving me insane.
There's gulag in the vegetables & gulag in the soap,
gulag likes to play the game of gulag-on-a-rope,
there's a gulag in my bed at night & gulag in my dreams,
if I don't feed the gulag I hear gulag-monster screams.
The gulag says it loves me & heaves a gulag sigh,
if I can't love my gulag back I'm surely gonna cry.
There's gulag in the razorblades & gulag in the glass,
gulag in the novichok & gulag in the gas:
the cemetery's just another gulag in disguise,
gulag fun is waiting for you even when you die.
There're gulags deep down underground & gulags in the sky,
gulags gulags everywhere eternally supplied!
And a little gulag Jesus w/ a lucky gulag star,
& a gulag god who sees how very happy we all are.

Confessions of Living in Fire

(i.m. Tzvetan Todorov)

The Tao says, The Way that can be described
isn't the true way – but can it be truly
described? Evil from imposing good on others,
the sacrificial ritual of writing (Tsvetaeva):
"Who sees injustice in the fact my hands are raw?"

Hung from a nail w/ yr defeat still
growing inside you – in a part of the world where
complaining isn't permitted. "There're
many who pretend that canons are aimed at them,
when in reality they're the target
merely of opera glasses" (Brecht).

And though it has many eyes some of them must
sleep – intoxicated by rainfall &
beautiful sinking ships & all tomorrow's
just conditions. There's writing on the wall, too,
but you'd think it was ancient Egyptian.

The Furniture of Home

Starker than the filament moon their wild bodies –
the closet rooms it was unbearable to leave

were mountains built-over by a sea,
a procession of fetishes between "them" & "it."

Because even the poem is a gutted impermanent thing
you've stuffed yr unwilling doppelgängers into

& like underwater islands they return laboriously
as drawn knots, as transplanted follicles

turned to basalt, lathed by fingers infantile & lithe
as carved syrup. And are the fault's they've loved

any less proverbial? Though you've heard it break
you too are no more continent than a tricked scale,

a drowned sun tattooed on an eye, or a man
crushed by a wave years before it reaches him.

Custodial Sentences

1. Left on a mountainside the little ones
still have a way of returning –
the perilous exile, the drowned rat
washed-up at the frontier post,
choleric rumours of life-to-come.
Impatient for the test of time they ran
every gauntlet, fame coveted them –
a moment's inattention & history
if it blinked wld never know what
buried it. And all this from the ratio
of a world's circumference? There never was
an insignificant thing, nor absolute.
Happiness is power's monotonous lullaby
dreaming the Esperanto of defeat.

2. A line drawn in sand
ants clockwise as in class struggle
my dear anachronism – the lone
merely stylise a person in lockdown theory
when they are less individual than
subdivided. Placed & re-
placed by fractious time, in-weighing
or inveighing, as if to de(s)ign
a *form of justice* – & strung it
atop a flagpole dialling sunless hours.
If an ant cld know the difference
between a mountain & a heap of rhetoric.
Life imitates life in order to survive
or for the sheer dumb expectation of it.

3. The same passion of time as when first
bled through / already silence grows
nostalgic for the creature
cunningly upsetting the traps / footprints
on the moon / an A-Z of infectious unease.
Extinction wipes its nose
in these bright cold uncalendared days —
memoirs of a cloned photofinish / the original
carbon copy rendered anxiously illegible
in homage to the Grand Mal. These & other
impersonated talismans of Art or Law:
"certain eternal things uttered for the last time."
As if, to relinquish the confines / whose
dust is no more eventual than Sisyphus.

4. It darkens over / god's witness
delivers the ultimatum: they are
shouting in tongues they are
erupting behind the blank screen.
All tomorrow's flagwaving entertainment
will have you in stitches —
an immigration cop's tears,
choruses of the epochally sanctified.
Another stanza of perpendicular talk:
the search for meaning in inter-
planetary leaps & bounds, god
is a mineral deposit on an asteroid.
Let us give thanks to those who live
so that we no longer have to.

5. Because the seasons failed to arrive that year
Earth stood still. Contagion was
a narcoleptic in a ventilated coffin –
House of Hammer reruns of Edgar Allan Poe.
What next: would afterlives be foisted
upon even the disbelieving?
There were questions to be asked but only
sentimental attachments to reply with.
Seizing the means of production
required too many definitions:
future prospects were as good
as a day of reckoning – but who would?
There'd be time to breathe afterwards, they
said, watching blue skies yawn over them.

Jaime Ramón Mercader

A room becomes its own exile fewer enter
till at last the deniable assassin.
Grass grows under his feet, ceilings yawn:
the anatomy of a freeze-frame describes
a ruined arc. Zeno's Paradox
isn't a paradox but the impossibility
of accomplished revolution.
Only an idiot believes they're a free
agent of the Will-to-Power.
Or the described arc interrupts its
Faustian progress to become
an interrogative corpse confronting
the shadow of a man who refuses to exist.
Even w/ crude doses of optimism
History isn't required to stomach its
just desserts. But is the bitter pill more
palatable, garnished w/ merchandise?

Angelus Novus

midnight & the shunting yard's musical spheres –
there's more than one extinction playing out
beyond the wire – under the lighthouse eye –
shaving bedrock from its cubist underlay to feel
w/ unconscious fingertips the trembling *eidos*.

in a graph of space & time – converging at zero
as at a border post in the Pyrenees –
depiction is like a blind Icarus-child abducted
to the mythical sunbird's Siberian nesting site.
foreshortened beyond perspective's reach –
wanting to outlive oneself is such a fiasco.

even w/ nobody to turn & face it
there's still an image of what isn't there
to wrestle w/ its furies in a rattling imperfect cage.
elements concealed are elements consoled
by hands at a task abstractly calibrating.
there's the door, it shuts w/out you.

even an escape-artist is expected to derive
a "mature style." wax melts – the ash-in-yr-eye look
turns deadpan – lean years fatten under pretence
to gravity. nostalgic for ineffables this
telescope sky yearns for the bottom of a well.
when the poem ends only the occasion dies.

"The European"

(for Ann Vickery)

I retrace the steps, adjust the experiment, discover
the secular & elemental co-ordinate.
This place to which the years had delivered him.
A prison-thin hand-rolled cigarette —
closed his right eye & stared at it.
Smelled of the old times. Brown dim skies
in an overcoat with swamped shoulders.
I stir crumbs of burnt toast into his tea —
a lukewarm plastic spoon — it is a kind of evidence,
an anagnorisis. Naming it would be useless.
He looks away as I clutch in vain —
the walls, the mirror behind the lunch counter.
First, because everything is form. Second,
by a redundant precision. The dissection scar
invisible behind the ear, for instance.
Guilt before recognition? Half-mocking he fell,
his lips, his feet, he was the paper tablecloth,
the parting sea. I see it all exactly. Each word exactly.
This predilection, like a cyst — every effort at affirming
turns to retaliation. The dislocated "stuck
moment." We arrive at the necessary
disorder by a voluble tomography.
Lying there, sitting, standing, stirring the tea the crumbs,
a swallowing of tongues, I also, I fall I retrace,
needle-eyed. A line with points distributed
on either side — a look, an unlook. And spent the better
part of his days escaping from that picture.

Monet, Trouville
("je suis décidément un imbécile")

A sea of holes – measured in time
from here to #35 boulevard des Capucines
sinuous red before kodachrome
in a tipped vase.
           All the separate
dancing threads of an eye too close
to the sun – presage Novembers
of desolation, the grey shore
freighted w/ debris of yet more
ancient wars to come.
           Or a disassembled
lightbulb occultly arranged around
the green holes in a blue tablecloth –
signifying a view from Manhattan
before skylines & *Das Kapital*.
           If the mined
Atlantics of separation fabled us
then what's history? Turned
by unoiled wheels that shriek in a night
smothered by cretaceous foliage –
contemplating the evolutionary lilypond.

On the Death of Rupert Murdoch

eviction returns in a state of damage –
the aliveness of terrain even as it burns.
time is a product of error / strange attractors
loosening the grip in pastiched alienisms –
one depthless surface on another
depthless surface. the unloved characteristic
goes to extremes / to claim worlds beyond quest / ion
pulled from background check / to be the thing
that can't be anything else. running through all of it
this reeling dis / possession / before / at the outset
the rules of State / an unstated con / stitution:
once "given" emphasis, wordlessness
becomes a birthright. to fake, entice, propel
e.g. the senses / concealment inserts small
fragments / vivisections, paranoias –
complex increments of police / of punctuation
being a matter of "life & death" in deepening
planes of near autism. possessive is nine-tenths
living &/or dead: please describe
in a manner befitting / e.g. extinct, perished –
what's aggregate by brunt of saying (?) / why not
insurrection (?) / cunning wheels machining the line
to stay warm burn metaphors or the
illusory representation of / politics
& hypothermia & pvc / one stage direction
fits all / the law how indeed a pig in shit

Escape from the Lucky Country

do not seek victory in small contentions — Khü Lí

Within a great nation's literature there are
hard & brutal refugees from
normalisation, drowning in white reems of legalese.
Kati Thanda is not a dead heart
("in the water the body is cultivated") –
only echoes make use of language
where permission demands a catechism.
                    All benign encrypted pathways
running lightless through the blackout –
how to segregate
one plagiarism from the next? Trilobites
buried in a cliff of makeshift space
& fickle cancel-shaped sepsis stuttering down
from mound-springs to shores
as fatalistic as they are
fail to constitute a property rite.
                    If fiction shows counter-claims –
exchanged for a few additions of exportable rarity
e.g. for "bauxite" read "death in custody" –
do the forbidden speak
only when in violent opposition?
(Modesty burns to listen.) Ever since Hegel
truth burrowing through the mind
is more than a floating star less than a yam flower.

The Disavowed [Portrait of Hans Natschke]

                    even a controlled lack of implication –
to retract an eye & draw him objectively half-formed:
face without mouth, the accentuated
golden mean? staring at a bowl of fruit
till it withers – till the worms turn.
For example, Günter Grass's *letter from an Israeli,*
born in Danzig, who asks for a Jewish section –
"very small" – in the German cemetery in Gdańsk…
In other words, it's not only a question of walls:
walls that wait to be abolished (like a
confronting witness?) – no, they're only walls,
they pretend to be only walls. Because
you want to see him only as he appears, as he begins
to appear, *from History.* Two hemispheres, two minds
disguised in the shape of a man, in a room, far
from forced evacuations, against a window onto a
construction site. Is it enough? The poem
like a rickety frame thrown up around all of this,
unable to bear the slightest weight.
In other words, it's not only a question of wills,
but of a loss of implication: *they're only words,*
they pretend to be only words. Reminding, as they must,
no matter how much each bends to our purpose.

Nostalgia is an Illness like any Other

In broad daylight slung across it –
smokestack, silos,
a shafthead buried between tracks.
Like misplaced dolmens.
You're still there
treading water in the brown hole under the bridge,
the face at the door, two coal-seam eyes.
Rain makes slanted lithographs on the sky,
a bore pump marks time.
I settle down to wait, for the long-jawed
kazoo boy pacing the corn furrows,
footsteps on the bell porch.
You also, in the front room,
lifting yr shirt over yr head,
were never as literal as these are.
Evening drizzles down,
climbs in by the window – the gashed flywire –
pawing the nocturnal furniture.
Everything twice
because invisible then that now, pedantically, insists.
Failing by not forgetting.
The whispered harangue,
the hand against the sheets –
a dog muttering stanzas in its sleep –
the hypnotic recession of railheads that don't exist.

2 Stanzas (for Gig Ryan)

imprimatur before its time
cons a vice –
getting nostalgic for last drinks, freedom was
the coincided dream she
polishes like
a saint at breakfast

in turn, undiagnosed visions
run rampant –
the penultimate hook, the co-
habited skin:

        shipping out,
        keel-jammed,

                in search of
                less
                republic solitudes

"Philosophy Has No Shadow"

Then forgetting refers above all / to the nurturing
of pain – being mercilessly subject.
An open window a blackbird / sun in its beak
alive with anatomic fire
& night under wing –
schedules & seasons in disarray.
One cultivates the sublime the way
the other cultivates fair weather.
Extinguishing suns hoist from sprung traps
explain nothing about the "death of god."
But is the bird in the song
as the song is in it? The window –
the more it gains in analgesic?
Let sleeping contradictions lie
(intractable as an eye's rapt insomnia).
Once a bird dreamt upon a windowsill / a strange
quotidian worm – it turns
& the pejorative world turns with it.
Behind its eye a mind darkly beating
lays a black obsidian egg.

Variations on a Luckless Country

1. Teeth in a jar, corks screwed to
arthritic fists. Creatured
from this vanishing lagoon –
a ten-mile stretch
of frozen sky reflected in it.
They stoop there, anchored,
boy & old man pocketing scrap
from the condemned lot.
It's not what was promised, but there's a pattern in it:
an interior surface

> gazetting the solemn
> high reverence
> of the late lamented.

Putting on the glad rags,
wowsers fluff their wings on the powerlines,
eyes out for a chance at a dog's dinner.
The beseeched world
extends a charitable view –
things construed as y'd construe a missing link,
a tribe of unhinged dressing-table mirrors.

> They're standing now
> at the lopsided front door.

>> One breath
>> & the whole
>> thing'll collapse.

2. Well they set up shop there 'cause all around was swamp-
infested, making a campfire of their one lifeboat
& kept watch from under the charred gunwale. Y'd've
mistook 'em all for Rabbis. And this was the grand
beacon-on-the-hill that squirt Austrayan w/ the turd
in his buttonhole was busy praising to the portside of Blighty.
(They knew a good thing when they could sell it cheap.)

It was time, all hands agreed, to found a new master race,
so one of them gold-panning yanks stuck a Wiradjuri girl
up a stag tree & they sat around downing turps while the march
of the black cockatoos dressed them in feathers & buckshot
& silver raiment & made right royal bastards of the lot.

3. Who knows how long it lasts –
bringing in the salt harvest,
the waning species under a wire-frame moon,
life after the fact?

You lie there, a withered bathtub demagogue
dreaming a swansong's bought encore.
Television. The cosmic dark horse
hanged w/ a two-dollar belt.

One last unbearable meal –
the man in the Houdini mindtrap,
the matchstick tower, the smear on the
sidewalk. Let these be warnings

to children weaving fairyfloss from yr hair.

Spectral teeth grind out 4 a.m. soliloquies.
The Indian Summer that year
stalked them more abjectly than ever.

4. In the dead of night – creeping up to the bar
at the Australia Hotel

like a Burma Railroad demolition crew.
Another April fool

on a three-week binge, hoisting
the Southern Cross

& digging-in for a saga of recaps long as the Mekong,
taxing to a nation

w/ a five-minute attention span.
The night they burnt

the place down, tabloid photo-fit intaglios
of Australopithecus

w/ a lip stiffened by a piece of four-by-two:
Such is life, they chimed,

sensing the moment was historical. The closing-time
referendum declared

an anti-republic six generations antique
bred from Bex powders

& fluked sheep. The fire brigade rang the anthem
through the streets,

the Unknown Soldier wept. Hearing a parade
was in the offing,

the whole town lined up for miles around,
just for the chance to piss on it.

Creeley in Mallorca

Why does a magician move his hands?
The ugly coffee-pot is the sea.
Beckoning between two opponents,
one perceives in the circumference of the other
an island. On its leeward
time is an updraught –
before Roman, Moorish, Aragonese.
Fish through hollow eyes observe
the swimming boy turn circles around the waves.
Will the angry coffee spoons
declare an emergency before the arrival of the alka-seltzer?
Will the boy outgrow the tide?
Grey patrol boats recite from afar
our schoolteachers' solemn credo.
Spaceships from Mars. The poem limping to conclusion.
Only what has sufficiently suffered should be
sufficiently cured, the old man said.

Kennst Du die Stadt am Bernsteinstrand?

Now I'm not alone w/ my near dead ones, insulated
in clockwork moronic sleep. The diligent insulins, the cruxes –
I reach across to bear up against them, pointing, a map,
a city abolished beneath a finger: it's child's play, they
want to catch you red-handed. Waiting in a line 44 years long,
it comes, too quickly, always, almost always –
an inspiration, a telephone, all it needs is the correct
receiver, der Zeit. Hurry up! If only by association, if only
as an accessory, they said, to his mother's fathers, etc. –
pronouncing the sentence upon the present arraignment…
(But you don't even speak their language!) It came
from before, w/ the omniscience of a secret file:
the picture, the baby on its back, hands, feet & scrotum.
Do you deny that's you? They're waiting
in the next room, the spools twitching, the needles.
Refusing to know I confess – that guilty you may steal forth
to be born, against the odds, wide eyed in place of me.

The House of the Suicide
& the House of the Mother of the Suicide
(on John Hejduk's monument to Jan Palach)

The Divided Man burned in the cold that burned his skin –
circling the square where he'd stood on his head
all his life,
                          a wet cigarette, a lurching
canine scent & gasoline & ozone &
through the park & all the streets & judas holes
& shopping bags & bloated feet
among ordinary people asleep w/ their mouths open,
mirrors & domestic violence in rooms of submerged feeling
& all tomorrow's calamities –

or there aren't any rooms only alternative facts,
as there are many facets to any one thing:
the erupted stage of a moon-rocket
escaping one gravity to be ensnared by others –
but such wonders were yet to come.

Bacchanalia

Morning orbits in its drone, a cloud in the shape
of a fly buzzing on a shadow-screen. Afghanistan
or a 20-year ad break. Between unsound & unheard,
certain genital sensations, melatonin, lying still
refusing to admit the Eros of their ways:
"Love of vanished epochs intensifies the illusion."
Now aghast before Time (the naked, post-partum
dictionary tone, future's afterlife) ex-
plaining how humiliation, too, has its place
in the heart – like the ventricle, the aorta,
a bird singing in a cake. *Oh cosmos who art
in thy egg!* Around the nucleic void, running yellow
up the astronaut's fork. (Who spies w/ infidel eye
the atomist's floating harem?) First rumours are
invariably sentimental. Though we are made of
sterner stuff, riding the Valkyries on a Victory Day
merry-go-round. Rank & file of dissected fish-heads
on vinegared newsprint. The map is more
than the territory, less than an erogenous zone.
Contoured like memory foam. Salted in the blood,
their wildest nights wld always be still to come.

Véronique à Vauvenargues

(for Véronique Vassiliou)

The blindwomen & the riddle of the elephant –
hung from the ceiling
like shorthand, a grain of truth
upsetting Paradise.

They are animating beneath the skin –
camera obscuras on a zoological theme.
(Barely imagined creatures
standing on their heads!)

Flattery again demands everything.
Savagery becomes us.

Let the world this afternoon abolish itself
a little less righteously:
a poem isn't an escape
to the antipodes of classification –
nor an immemorial elephant
in the proverbial room.

Because otherwise only foregone conclusions.

Here the unwelcome creature sits
w/ strange & awkward grace
patiently unriddling
its elaborate counterproof,
till the whole comes blatantly into view.

Ḥaġar Qim

Once more the world hangs in the balance –
& like clockwork you lie blushing
in a field of stones – strawman
sobbing into yr breasts, crows
in the clouds, the orphanage
on the hill.
                Picture a landscape
in which no-one's buried – no ebb
flow of soap sellers, or the abstracted
waltz around the boards, of raisons d'être
w/ sheared goats' tails.

Blood-laughter, interjected w/ all
the summary gravitas of Heinrich Himmler
attempting the Resurrection Cakewalk –
you switch channels & a staged moonrocket
teeters in the sky.
              What the tribe demands,
you provide, in dreams that are
meanders of dust as upon some
quantum littoral, turned to a cinema
of abjurations:
                pedantic as phrenology –
sublime as an angular momentum
couched in poetry – or the pale god's
anti-semite grin, while it subtly fornicates.

That Happy Place

On the basis of a missed opportunity: watchtowers
teetering into the waves, the crisis of day's end.

Was this the price of a lungful of air?
Between the inner form & its outer dimensions

the river swells against the locks, the grass
lies down under the rain, all more or less patiently.

Others wait asquat the rain-dark sand
their guts spilled in pointless endeavours.

Like a paroxysm left to rot. And we who've prayed
to the myth of a coordinated response, to be

that shiftless pivot, lean & fastidious
as a godhead in uniform, flexing its loins,

assured that time & also gratitude are unending.
For years almost nothing, then suddenly the scornful

leap out the window, the camera framing
a tight close-up on the back of yr head.

Dirty dishes in the kitchen sink, phantasmagoric
interior lives poured out openly like algebra

or sex objects or chemotherapy. The watchers make
every ulterior inch a tranquillised allure of punct-

iliousness or something even they don't have words for.
As if all this did shine w/ intrinsic light,

the live part of it gasping for mythological oxygens,
present yet still inchoate? Now you are drawn up

into the symbolic opposite, to be a straight line
towards that perennially deliberate plane.

Even in isometric grey the secret appraisals
tip their hands, the exhumation party setting out

upon the reefs, where death lies hidden
like the parts of prudery from less strident ardours.

New World Capitalism
(for Martin Langford)

Some revolutionaries can't help themselves. Contemptuous
of meaning, the appalled imagination seeks emergence:
oxygen, as a socially useful substance. It does this now.
Sucking the frozen cornucopia in high-pitched bafflement,
all happy cordials leached away. You draw a line,
a coiling escape-trajectory from any outback Martian town
to wherever you dream of being. Money comes in
different shades, receding further & faster. In specimen jars
they collect many joyless flies, snared on webs of
unlanguaged randomness. The secret was to live off the land
like a spider forced to fend for itself in zero gravity.
Are these "unrelated facts" unrelated? The million watchers
saw shadowy figures, clumsy in appearance, yet strangely
graceful in movement, weaving the lattice of coincidence:
it was a day of miracles, of telephones ringing. At last
the moment of confrontation arrived, staring into fistfuls of
red dust. "We come in peace," they said, demanding a receipt.

Europe in Its Time

When the lion was cut open, there was a hive of bees,
hunter-gatherer semaphores on a gold plate, the great
TV in the sky, thought balloons, a single origin.
But our wandering lights are not the cynosure, we are
the product of dead ends where many languages
spoke. Even the most fervent is a temporary ziggurat,
haemoglobins of deep spiritual intent, the solar diocese
of barbaric heliums. Like watching yr hair fall out.

Because we are interpenetrated beings, our makers
regale us w/ plastic fruit, reasoning the conspicuous alibi,
the snake in the grass, the pleasures of self-appeasement.
The next crisis proves its point, launching the ships
for the sake of the franchise – blood moons ornamenting
a holographic sky petrified in amber celluloid.

Postcard from Elsewhere

Mañana's another day. Time to shut the window, split the
difference, beat the piñata. A wave's always rising
whenever you look & even when you don't. Nine minutes
to ten to eleven to midnight. Did one require the other?
I believe I don't believe. *Ich glaube ich glaube nicht.*
Children barefoot running in flooded hallways –
to weave backwards the pattern of their undoing.
His fingernails were cracked. TV crews in expectation of
ratings catastrophe. Happiness, my love, was no longer
having to dream about you. A dog under the tarmac,
the cobbles beneath the sand. Blindmen w/ machetes
hack coconuts while smiling at you, biding their time.
The sky's leaking again, the crew bails faster then slower:
everything that hasn't happened could still be "yet to come."
You've painted yr glasses black. The Blue Danube.
The Green Green Grass of Home. Mama's knocking
at the window again – did you brush yr teeth before doing
anything blameworthy? Oh the people here are beautiful,
they look nothing like you.

Statue of Svatopluk Čech, Pond w/ Fountain

freefall to swoop or trip-up aerofoiled
alighting dusk a square pane liquid
in head-shimmer drinks itself dry –
the industrious magpie deciphers the waterclock:
is this where naming begins
possessing a method?
far from the bellicose deserts
of nationalismus –
the poem defies gravity insouciant
as a waterspout.
here the bounding black wolf-pelt muzzles the ball.
all for joy of repetition
& repetition for all!
love begins w/ an insurrectionary mirror –

> turning corners midair
> these unsuspected qualities
> because taken as given
> where most are not.

Return to the You-Beaut Country (for John Olsen)

…which among other benefits will change the taste of the sea & disperse
or precipitate bituminous particles by spreading a boreal citric acid…

— Charles Fourier

lying on their backs
pissing into the
lemonade sky,
the hidden persuaders
sang their innocence

it was springtime at 3 o'clock
a crab-eyed
blue anus on a stalk –
passionate aerosols
were god's last-known abode

moratorium w/out faces.
an aggregate
of responseless units
whited by salt-haze

the mirror runs backwards
across sand dunes in which
the day-to-come
was buried w/out trace

Prehistoric Rock Pictures

Fairly soon the fog will clear – the abandoned countryside,
the jutting balconies, the ambivalent volumetric mouth
forming a concentric target. Far simpler than it seemed,
once there were no more unbearable reels to play.
Driving through a night familiar from black-&-white TV
reruns, the fusion sequence w/ page numbers memorised.
Equally there was no light in which to receive instructions:
porous & rocklike, the unexpected rigours of a censored line.
In Technicolor, the key to the collective insoluble dream –
& now we have to hear all about the Author's intestinal
complaint. The lymphatic brain, unfound for centuries,
began showing up emphatically in all the queerest places.
A pair of at-first-glance enamelled eyes, an embryonic
gill-slit, a half-coloured mermaid in a child's doodle-book.
The Central Committee ordered the nonintersecting time-
frames to intersect – do they deserve such scorn? Do you?
Another unseasonal storm turning everything grey.
Slipping out unseen from adjacent situations, whose
martyrology are we composing now Monsieur Artaud?
As an instance, pitched inside its breath, isn't a voice,
so the expired celluloid cast shadows of doubt on the
mouth as the child kissed it. The entire police force
looked inside to see if there was anyone still alive in there –
joyous as an ochre sky crucified on spears of dusking light.
When nothing was left to eat he retired to write his
long-awaited manifesto – it was the moment the aliens
chose to invade, scaling a state-of-the-art periscope from
the Great Crevasse, armed to the teeth w/ archetypes.
"We are among you," the chalked semaphore on the child's
doorstep said. Spacemen in mail-order plastic sachets,
all they required was the addition of water, oceans of it.
Years later, listening to rain on foreign windowsills at night:
each time you opened yr eyes innocents suffered.

Eventually the censors would be forced to break cover & act
"in the public good" – Laurel-&-Hardy figures making
choreographed footprints on the moon, planting god's own
flag for TV proletariats grown accustomed to advertising.
Impaired by amorousness, wheeled creatures disported
in the streets, till dawn found them exhausted & supine.
What would come of this world when the next one died?
Optimistically he caressed w/ dental floss each morning
before a mirror – another peninsular missile crisis had
kept him from sleep, thinking how untold rare, the Earth,
if only there were some real connoisseurs left to sell it to.
Little pieces of dialectic floated in a cocktail glass –
tasted sweet – the quartet, on the other hand, a single note
arranged in complex manifolds. The instalment plan
promised unfettered billboard views at a premium –
now that their dream was on the verge of fulfilment.
Did their possessions love them as much as *they* did?
History, the Author explained, was a metaphor for un-
diminished replay potential, the task of life being
just what it said it was. Obviously another crank w/ an
axiom to grind. Never _____ a gift-horse in the mouth,
was an unwavering conviction they'd been carrying around
since birth – before mythical beings became plentiful.
Rumour had it that left to its own devices humanity
wld've preferred a career in orthodontics. By stages
the mechanism stripped itself of inessentials, beginning
w/ the occipital cavity. Is that where ideas come from?
Knowing that every ridiculous question has its twin
somewhere in the universe, keeping the Big Picture
synchronised. If enough circumstances conspired
perhaps they wldn't need people anymore but who wants
to be admired by machines? God's bespoke love-doll
was programmed to perform 40 kinds of euthanasia.
Would Marathon Man get his moment in the sun?
They built this city on AIDS & inflation-adjustment,

then changed the names, but we still remember them.
A charitable view isn't the cynical acme it appears,
as when the camera pans across a harbour decked-out
in carnival lights, at the approaching glacier.

The Plague Tree (i.m. Nanni Balestrini)

On Ermanno Olmi's *L'Albero degli zoccoli* (1978)

1. What shall we do w/ the bodies?

2. Leaves in the wind. Machines. Insects. Birds. Voices in the leaves. Believe & be silent. God prates through the hours & miles, interpellating their crimes. A pastoral. Headless on the block, the quacking ideologue. The tree sings, laughs, pukes. Habeas corpus bound hand & foot among the branches. Strange fruit. Sexless as a crude handmade wooden fetish. All creation raining down. Flyblown in the seedbeds' humus mulch slime. In the sentimental camera-eye making a landscape of it. Work, boredom, fatigue. Of those who suffer, alone collectively. Of those who obey. Of those who are permitted to obey.

3. The first commune is the ditch they throw the corpses of the poor in.

4. La bella figura (strategia della tensione):

fig. 1.   "Operazione Piave": a Wehrmacht soldier guarding the bodies of 31 local partisans hanged from trees along the Corso Centrale, Bassano del Grappa, 26 September 1944

fig. 2.   The corpses of Benito Mussolini & Clara Petacci alongside other executed fascists in Piazzale Loreto, Milan, 28 April 1945, hung upsidedown on meathooks from the metal girder framework of a half-built Standard Oil service station

fig. 3.   Giuseppe Penone, *Pietra corda, albero, sole/Pietra, corda, albero, proggia* (*Stone, rope, tree, sun/Stone, rope, tree, rain*), 1968

fig. 4.   Giuseppe Penone, *Alpi Marittime* (*Maritime Alps*), 1968

fig. 5.   The body of Aldo Moro – shot eleven times in the chest by Mario Moretti, head of the Brigate Rosse, after 54 days in captivity – discovered in the boot of a red Renault IV on Via Caetani, Rome, midway between Christian

Democratic Party & Communist Party headquarters, 19
March 1978

5. Y're in bed, y're neither awake nor asleep. Night grazes yr neck
w/ its teeth. It wants to suck yr blood, but first it's going to play a
little. Turn you into a picture for the watchers on the other side of
the screen. A voluptuous, forensic victim drowning in the unsleep
they've created for you. Dreaming of them, always, on the occasions
y're allowed to dream at all. Mechanics of god's impermeable will.
Desolate angels of release. How nakedly y've served them. Sun-up
to sundown like the walking dead. *Because we need this to survive.*

6. The task of the colonizing forces isn't to occupy the territory but
the unconscious of its inhabitants.

7. Dark beasts feasting on a moonlit carcass. Lunatics, werewolves,
menstrual cycles. *It is the moon that guides the Wanderer through her
metamorphoses.* Born from water, one arm raised above its head. The
figure hanged in the tree becomes the tree. Just as the poet brings
to radiance the filth of despair. For a few hours more, a buried
level of paradox turned into a thing. A bleeding heart. A whole
reliquary. Despite the abundance of the image, all it signifies is a
scarcity of meaning. Scarcity born of the politics of scarcity.

8. Exiled in the wilderness, which will run out first?

9. *"Those lacking imagination take refuge in reality."* (Godard)
Worked to death in the construction of its disappearance, the
earth sprouts a giant hologram. An invisible Reign of Terror.
Soylent generic. Fissile antimatter. Void. Wrapped in polyurethane,
history's corpse. Exhausted. Disenchanted. Fed up. After the years
of lead. A tree petrified from its ontology. Indentured. Obsolete. A
petrified image. Grown devout in the presence of its own poverty.

10. The course of the seasons is spent, now there is only the course
of power.

fig. 1

fig. 2

fig. 3

fig. 4

fig. 5

Destitution

The legislative power of the Commonwealth shall be vested...

born where it doesn't elect / to acquire less than a right-of-refusal
/ though not all are strangers in this room not all in the room are
seen / vision splendid pumped full ~~of holes~~ / *till by effect a bloody
cause is known* / out of the cradle solemnly rocking a timebomb to
sleep / who'll know the hour for which it's set? / untreated they
lie w/ one ear to the ground the other to the telephone / & what
of the ancient mystic poem that mandrake-like shrieks alarm?
/ do great deeds die more than metaphor's death? / for every
crime a plagiarist commends themselves to posterity / but to a
mind as exposed as the exposed bed of an inland sea & in such a
state / "disordered" / raving about ghostships in a desert 50,000
years before cinema? / & so erect their blank slate / *but shalt thou
save alive nothing that breaths*? / deliberately because neither wealth
nor acquisitiveness / despite boundarylines / procedures / too
many miscellaneous / loose threads in mock-Bayeux (trademark
pending) / & if the offence be not committed within? / the
singing stones tell litigation's fortune / made saleable art from
x-ray bodies in Sisyphus stress-position / A-bomb silhouettes /
shouldering this red rock up a gradient to stake claim over stacked
odds / but language comes from other worlds half-hidden by
false nature like a sphinx in the mountains / it whispers & out
fly the deities of plundered realestate / over continents dark w/
iconoclast debris / sauve qui peut! / & all equal under the sign of a
hung albatross / being the redemption of a criminal enterprise by
a lunatic's decree / & so the beast its requisite judicial mannerism
/ eye for incremental eye / tooth for ravenous denture / progress
only counts by ratios / & for the sake of theories bled white (every
word its own petard) knowingly / the molecular clock runs down
in mimicked vacancy / here monopoly begins / Q: how long is an
invasive species? / red spider-mites in arid conditions proliferate /
decimated foliage a readymade heraldry / magnetised northsouth
in quarter-acre subplots (whodunit?) / bootjacking in lockstep /

those enterprising denominators' courage of conviction / one joke redeems another / like an unread crime haunting the bestseller list / ("but officer…") / 252 days out of Portsmouth / bound to a Botany Bay whippingpost for the illumed panopticorp's deportment lesson / *miserable you miserable me miserablest of the Earth are we!* / touched by gawd their mad ayatollah naked down corridors / enfilades / where rain falls mainly on the chief protagonist / an atmospheric river / chained Wandjina avatars / History's sublime tabula rasa glows in its Mercator cage / mistaken for some rare object of morphosyntactic research / whitewashed piecemeal vivisection / their Via Gloriosa (AUSTRAYA DRIVE IT LIKE YOU STOLE IT) makes poetries of sacrament / as upon this or any other day the nay-saying carnival of traffic noise going round on the Big Carousel / goading the Big Eye to vertigo / the gavelling Big Wig / or a mown lawn's secret prospect onto Paradiso for all buried beneath / sunk into the mouthless well of itself / freefall or freeforall / as when first expeditionaries shunted into caves by mountainous sea-voice / & lay an absence of light upon the walls / as one lays hands on the ceremonial body / in place of the living body / pigmented in braille / hypoxic ochres awash in fear & revelation & points of no return.

www.ingramcontent.com/pod-product-compliance
Lightning Source LLC
Chambersburg PA
CBHW030843090426
42737CB00009B/1093